# the Music of Life

### Bartolomeo Cristofori &
### the Invention of the Piano

by Elizabeth Rusch

illustrated by Marjorie Priceman

Atheneum Books for Young Readers
New York   London   Toronto   Sydney   New Delhi

ATHENEUM BOOKS FOR YOUNG READERS
An imprint of Simon & Schuster Children's Publishing Division
1230 Avenue of the Americas, New York, New York 10020

ATHENEUM BOOKS FOR YOUNG READERS
is a registered trademark of Simon & Schuster, Inc.
Atheneum logo is a trademark of Simon & Schuster, Inc.
For information about special discounts for bulk purchases, please contact
Simon & Schuster Special Sales at 1-866-506-1949 or business@simonandschuster.com.
The Simon & Schuster Speakers Bureau can bring authors to your live event.
For more information or to book an event, contact the Simon & Schuster Speakers Bureau at 1-866-248-3049
or visit our website at www.simonspeakers.com.
Book design by Debra Sfetsios-Conover
The text for this book is set in Goudy Oldstyle Std.
The illustrations for this book are rendered in gouache and ink.
Manufactured in China
0117 SCP
First Edition
2 4 6 8 10 9 7 5 3 1
Library of Congress Cataloging-in-Publication Data
Names: Rusch, Elizabeth, author. | Priceman, Marjorie, illustrator.
Title: The music of life : Bartolomeo Cristofori and the invention of the piano / Elizabeth Rusch ;
illustrated by Marjorie Priceman.
Description: First edition. | New York : Atheneum Books for Young Readers, [2017]
Identifiers: LCCN 2015017472
ISBN 978-1-4814-4484-2
ISBN 978-1-4814-4485-9 (eBook)
Subjects: LCSH: Cristofori, Bartolomeo, 1655-1732—Juvenile literature. | Harpsichord makers—Italy—
Biography—Juvenile literature. | Piano makers—Italy—Biography—Juvenile literature. | Piano—History—
18th century—Juvenile literature.
Classification: LCC ML3930.C923 R87 2017 | DDC 786.2/19092 [B]—dc23
LC record available at https://lccn.loc.gov/2015017472

To all the music makers

–E. R.

May 6, 1655, Padua
"Bartolomeo, son of Francesco Christofani and of Luara his wife,
was baptized by me, Don Gagliardi his parish priest."
—*Baptismal record, Church of St. Luke*

## Pianissimo (very soft)

IN PADUA, Italy, Bartolomeo Cristofori's home since his birth, a hush envelops the room as the instrument maker carefully adjusts the tuning pins of a clavichord. Feet pad across the room. Cloth rustles. Sand falls silently through an hourglass.

Cristofori treasures the quiet so he can coax just the right notes from the delicate instrument. He strikes a key firmly, and inside the clavichord a small metal strip presses a string. A pitch-perfect *pianissimo* note trembles out. In the garden, starlings chatter, nearly overpowering the soft sound.

# crescendo (becoming louder)

Outside, a parade of pounding hooves and clattering wooden wheels grows closer and closer, louder and louder. Horses whinny, snort, and stamp as a young prince and his entourage spring from the carriages to the cobblestones.

*His Highness Prince Ferdinando de Medici!*
Word of Cristofori's gift for tuning and restoring keyboard instruments has spread throughout the land. The prince, an accomplished musician, has come to examine Cristofori's work for himself.

"[Prince Ferdinando] played various instruments to perfection, but the harpsichord as a great master. . . ."
—*History of the Noble and Royal House of the Medici*

Cristofori shows the prince to a harpsichord, a keyboard instrument that plucks stiff strings. Ferdinando sits and begins to play. *Forte* notes, strong and loud, ring out.

Prince Ferdinando yearns for his court to become the musical center of Italy. He urges Cristofori: Come to Florence. Join my court.

Cristofori is torn, reluctant to leave the peace of Padua.

1709
"The prince was told that I did not wish to go; he replied that he would make me want to."
—*Notes of Scipione Maffei from his interview of Bartolomeo Cristofori*

8

## crescendo

(becoming louder)

But the prince makes an offer Cristofori cannot refuse: a house complete with all the furnishings he could need, generous pay—12 *scudi* a month—and an important position, Master Instrument Maker and Tuner.

Best of all, Cristofori would be able to work with the most elegant keyboards in Italy—and have the chance to build some beautiful new ones of his own.

So Cristofori sets off for Florence.

May 6, 1688, Florence
"To Bartolomeo Cristofori of Padova, new harpsichord maker to the Most Serene Prince Ferdinando: two pair of pine bed planks; two mattresses of cloth and hair . . . two bedcovers of red cloth . . . one copper kettle . . . three ladles and three forks, brass . . ."

—*Medici records*

# FORTISSIMO

(very loud)

When Cristofori arrives, he installs his worktable in the long row of the famous Medici workshops, alongside the most talented stone engravers, goldsmiths, lathe workers, tapestry weavers, and potters of the region. How different from his workshop at home! Wool beaters thump and looms clatter-clack. *KA-CHUNK* goes the printing press. The cabinetmakers saw and bang endlessly.

Cristofori can't hear himself think. Even worse, he can barely hear the instruments he is trying to tune. . . .

1709
"It was very tiring for him to be in the large room with this deafening noise. . . ."
—*Maffei's notes from his interview of Cristofori*

So Cristofori moves his workshop out of the hubbub and into his house. He planes boards and saws keys as a fire crackles in the hearth. He glues joints as tin plates clink in the kitchen. He tunes strings as a nearby fountain splashes joyfully.

Novemeber 4, 1693, Florence
"I, Bartolomeo Cristofori, claim from the Treasury of the Serene Prince Ferdinando of Tuscany . . . for remaking another harpsichord inlaid with ivory, ebony, and green marble . . ."

—*Medici records*

Bells toll and clang and chime, ringing in the dawns, the days, the
weeks, and the years as Cristofori restores sixteen of the prince's keyboard
instruments—and builds from scratch nine more.

The prince and the people of Florence find Cristofori's work to be masterful.
But for Cristofori, his creations are not good enough. The harpsichords and
clavichords he restores and builds can only do so much.

FORTE (loud)

For no matter how gently a musician presses the keys, when the harpsichord plucks its strings, the sound is loud, always loud.

And no matter how vigorously a musician presses the keys of the clavichord, when its tiny metal strips tap the strings, the sound is soft, so very soft.

Neither instrument can start *sotto voce* like the whispered gossip of neighbors and build to an angry argument. No one can play a pounding march, then drop down to a lovely lullaby. There's no way to surprise listeners with a few feathery or furious notes.

*mezzo piano* (moderately soft)

As Cristofori ponders this problem, he delivers harpsichords to the Medici's Pitti Palace, for concerts in the gardens. There, he marvels at great stone statues—how sculptors he once worked beside have brought marble to life!

August 12, 1690, Florence
"Owed to me, Bartolomeo Cristofori, by the Treasury of His Serene Highness, Prince Ferdinando of Tuscany for having a harpsichord moved twice to the Pitti Palace from my house . . ."

—*Medici records*

Cristofori lugs harpsichords to the prince's favorite villa outside the city, for concerts in the theater. There, he admires the prince's room of small paintings by great masters— how artists have evoked a moment in time with just color and lines!

Cristofori accompanies harpsichords to Pratolino, the prince's summer residence, for magnificent operas. There, Cristofori hears violins, violas, and voices rising from a hushed whisper to a bellowing bravado, capturing all a person can feel. How much can be expressed with stone and paint and bows on strings. If only Cristofori's keyboard instruments could so fully express the music of life!

The instrument maker yearns to create a new keyboard, one that can be played as softly as a gentle rain and as loudly as a booming thunderstorm.

But how?

1679, Pratolino
"The opera was rehearsed twenty-five times in all, two times with the instruments reinforced by the addition of keyboard. . . ."
—Ferdinando Luca

19

# crescendo
(becoming louder)

Cristofori wanders the streets and workshops of Florence. All around him hammers rise and fall. *Tink, tink* go the tiny hammers of the goldsmiths and silversmiths. *Tap, tap* the sculptor's mallet strikes. BANG, BANG the blacksmith's sledgehammer pounds.

Even in the piazzas, hammers dance above dulcimers, filling the air with a rich range of sounds.

Maybe hammers are the solution!

# mezzo forte

(moderately loud)

But what should the hammers be made of? Wood, paper, leather? Cristofori scours the bustling markets of Florence for a variety of materials. With the clink of gold florins, he pays the shopkeeper.

Back at his workshop, Cristofori wonders: What would be the best design for the hammers? He experiments, carving wood carefully. The hammers begin to take shape: wide at the base, narrow in the middle.

The hammers will strike stretched strings, he decides. But what kind of strings? Brass, steel, gut, or gold? The strings should be strong enough to endure pounding, but still vibrate richly.

For a warm, clear tone, he chooses brass and stretches the strings tightly across a strong cypress soundboard.

Now the instrument maker faces the toughest challenge of all: How can musicians change the volume simply by varying the pressure on the keys? Cristofori experiments with different ways for the keys to control how fast and how forcefully the hammers swing.

At first, the hammers strike too hard, breaking the strings. Then they tap too softly to be heard. They sometimes even rebound, striking the note twice.

Finally, Cristofori crafts a clever solution. Now pressing a key flings a hammer at the string. Immediately, the hammer falls back and is caught, poised to play again.

The inventor assembles a long row of keys, hammers, and strings in a sturdy wooden case.

Cristofori gazes at his masterpiece, which is covered in red leather, lined with green taffeta, and trimmed with gold ribbon. On the outside, it looks just like a harpsichord.

But inside is the marvelous new mechanism.

What will his patron think of it?

1700, Florence
"[A] new invention, that makes the *piano* and the *forte*, with . . . its red leather cover lined with green taffeta and hemmed with golden ribbon."
—*Medici inventory of instruments*

# Piano (soft)

*Finalmente!* In 1700, Bartolomeo Cristofori unveils his new invention. Prince Ferdinando sits before the instrument. He taps a key slowly and gently, and the sound is soft and sweet. He presses the keys harder and faster, and the notes ring out loud and clear. The prince plays a peaceful lullaby, a joyful jingle, a rollicking round.

"It is possible to play both *piano* and *forte*!" a court musician marvels.

The prince calls him a "virtuoso."

Cristofori bows, full of pride.

Cristofori's wonderful invention is eventually named for what it can do.

It is called . . . the pianoforte.

Cristofori is pleased, but he is not done. For years, he tinkers endlessly with his pianoforte, making the mechanism smoother and even more responsive.

But the keyboard is so sensitive, musicians struggle to play it. Hit a key a little too hard—DONG!—or too soft—*ding!*—and the volume follows. The more responsive Cristofori makes his instrument, the more reluctant musicians are to play it.

DONG
*ding*

Undaunted, Cristofori spends the rest of his long life perfecting his invention, coaxing it to respond precisely to a musician's touch. He hopes that someday, someone will use it to capture the music of life.

1711, Italy

"But truly, the major opposition that has been raised against this new instrument is the general lack of knowledge at first of how to play it. . . ."

—*Article by Scipione Maffei about Cristofori's pianoforte*

# Morendo

(dying away)

A few royal courts buy Cristofori's amazing pianoforte, but still the harpsichord reigns as the most popular keyboard in the land.

And before he is able to see his instrument embraced widely by musicians, Bartolomeo Cristofori dies in 1732 at the age of 76.

# dal niente (out of silence)

But Bartolomeo Cristofori's invention lives on. An article about his amazing instrument is published in Germany, and an organ maker there begins crafting pianofortes. The instrument slowly spreads across Europe.

1725, Germany
"Constructing [a keyboard] so that it might have this gift [of soft and loud could] be deemed . . . a vain endeavor. Nevertheless, such a bold invention has been no less happily conceived than executed, in Florence, by Signor Bartolommeo Cristofali."
—*Critica Musica*

# crescendo
## (becoming louder)

Musician Joseph Haydn tries a pianoforte for the first time.
Its responsiveness lights his imagination on fire.

"My imagination plays on me as if I were a
keyboard . . . I am really just a living keyboard."
—Joseph Haydn to biographer Albert Christoph Dies

In a concert in 1777, the young virtuoso Wolfgang Amadeus Mozart dazzles an audience with the instrument's expressive possibilities. From that moment on, Mozart and countless others compose all their keyboard music for the pianoforte.

*molto crescendo*
(becoming much louder)

October 28, 1777, Germany
"The rendering on the pianoforte was so neat, so clean, so full of expression, and yet . . . extraordinarily rapid . . . one hardly knew what to give attention to first . . . all the hearers were enraptured. . . ."
—*The Augsburg State*

# FORTISSIMO
(very loud)

Cristofori's invention, eventually called simply the piano, becomes a powerful tool in the hands of brilliant composers everywhere.

Ludwig van Beethoven's piano rings out, rousing and full of joy.

Johannes Brahms's piano soothes to sleep.

Scott Joplin's
piano dances.

Clara Schumann's
piano sings.

Claude Debussy's piano
makes moonlight.

And today, all around the world, in the hands
of countless musicians, young and old, Bartolomeo
Cristofori's piano captures the music of life.

# Time Line of the Life of Bartolomeo Cristofori and the Piano

**May 4, 1655:** Bartolomeo Cristofori is born in Padua, Italy.

**August 9, 1663:** Prince Ferdinando de Medici is born in Florence, Italy.

**February 1688:** The Medici family's harpsichord maker Antonio Bolgioni dies.

**March or April 1688:** Returning from Venice to Florence, Prince Ferdinando de Medici stops in Padua to invite Bartolomeo Cristofori to join his court.

**May 1688:** Cristofori is identified in Medici archives as the new instrument maker of the Serene Prince Ferdinando.

**1690:** Cristofori begins working out of his home in Florence.

**1690–1698:** Cristofori restores nine harpsichords, five spinets, and two organs, and builds two spinets, one organ, and six harpsichords. He transports instruments to and from his own house and Palazzo Pitti, Pratolino, and the prince's Poggio a Caiano villa.

**1700:** The first pianoforte, invented by Bartolomeo Cristofori, is described in an inventory of Medici instruments.

**1709:** Writer Scipione Maffei interviews Cristofori about his new invention, the pianoforte.

**1711:** Maffei publishes an article describing in detail Cristofori's pianoforte, including a complete diagram of the hammer mechanism.

**October 31, 1713:** Prince Ferdinando de Medici dies in Florence. Cristofori is later appointed *Custode* (keeper) of the Medici musical instruments by Ferdinando's father, Grand Duke Cosimo III. Cristofori continues making and selling pianofortes.

**1719:** Maffei publishes a new version of his article on Cristofori's pianoforte in his book *Rime e Prose*.

**1725:** Maffei's 1719 article on Cristofori's pianoforte is translated into German and published in the journal *Critica Musica*.

**January 27, 1732:** Bartolomeo Cristofori dies in Florence.

**1732:** Lodovico Giustini publishes six sonatas, the first music composed specially for the pianoforte.

**1732:** Gottfried Silbermann constructs his first pianoforte, most likely based on the German translation of Maffei's article or experience with a pianoforte made by Cristofori or one of his apprentices.

**1750:** Joseph Haydn plays his first pianoforte during his apprenticeship in Vienna at age twenty-eight.

**1768:** Johann Christian Bach performs a "Solo on the Piano Forte" in London.

**October 22, 1777:** Wolfgang Mozart plays a pianoforte at the concert hall of Count Fugger in Augsburg. All of Mozart's keyboard works composed after this concert were intended for the pianoforte.

**1780s and onward:** The pianoforte, soon known simply as the piano, overtakes the harpsichord in popularity. Composers such as Ludwig van Beethoven, Johannes Brahms, Frédéric Chopin, Clara and Robert Schumann, and Claude Debussy use the piano almost exclusively for keyboard compositions and performances.

**Today:** The piano is used worldwide to compose and perform a wide variety of music including classical, jazz, gospel, boogie-woogie, the blues, country, and rock.

# THE THREE SURVIVING CRISTOFORI PIANOS

No one knows how many pianofortes Bartolomeo Cristofori made in his lifetime, but some estimate close to twenty. Three survive, all built in the 1720s. Each pianoforte contains an inscription that translates roughly to "Bartolomeo Cristofori of Padua, inventor, made in Florence," with a date given in Roman numerals. Here are some more tidbits about these three amazing instruments, which have survived for close to three hundred years:

**The 1720 pianoforte** on display at the Metropolitan Museum of Art in New York City has fifty-four keys (four and half octaves). The instrument is playable, but the soundboard has been replaced, and other changes made have probably altered its sound.

**The 1722 pianoforte** housed at the Museo Nazionale degli Strumenti Musicali in Rome has forty-nine keys (four octaves). Its playing mechanism reflects improvement from the 1720 version, suggesting Cristofori continued to refine his instrument. This pianoforte has been damaged by worms and is not playable.

**The 1726 pianoforte** exhibited at the Musikinstrumenten-Museum at Leipzig University has forty-nine keys (four octaves) and is playable. The best-preserved of the three pianofortes, this one has the most sophisticated hammer mechanism. It is the closest surviving ancestor of the modern piano.

## Listening to Bartolomeo Cristofori's Pianofortes

Do you wonder what a pianoforte made by Bartolomeo Cristofori sounds like? You can listen to short clips of music played on original, restored, and replica Cristofori pianofortes on the websites of Italian-keyboard makers Kerstin Schwarz (animus-cristofori.com) and Denzil Wraight (denzilwraight.com/crisdisc.htm).

You can also hear what a clavichord sounds like here: youtube.com/watch?v=sbVILI4hJ9c And a harpsichord here: youtube.com/watch?v=GMoWNSP2gFk

# TODAY'S PIANO

Most of Cristofori's innovations live on in modern pianos. Key features of the pianoforte found in pianos today are:

- Wooden hammers strike metal strings.

- Dampers silence strings not being played.

- A mechanism amplifies the motion of the player's finger. (Every movement of the key creates eight times more movement in the hammer.)

- A mechanism rebounds the hammer after it strikes the string and catches it so that the hammer doesn't muffle the sound or restrike the string.

- The soundboard is isolated from the part of the piano that holds the strings so that the board vibrates more freely and creates a richer sound.

Still, modern pianos *do* sound different from Cristofori pianofortes thanks to a few improvements:

- Modern grand pianos have a broader range, eighty-eight keys (more than seven octaves) compared to Cristofori's forty-nine or fifty-four (more than four octaves).

- Iron bracing added to the design in the nineteenth century enables musicians to play the instrument much more loudly.

- Cristofori used brass strings. Modern pianos use steel. The steel strings are also thicker, so they can be strung more tightly. This allows the musician to hit the keys and strings harder, producing louder notes.

- Cristofori built in two strings for every note. Modern pianos vary the number of strings the hammers hit, from just one string per note in the lower bass, to two in the upper bass, and three in middle and upper ranges.

- Cristofori's hammer heads were made of rolled paper covered with cloth or leather. Modern hammer heads are made of wood and covered with felt.

This may seem like a lot of changes, but it's not. Today's piano reflects only minor improvements on Bartolomeo Cristofori's brilliant creation.

# Listening to the Music of Life

Many pieces of music rouse our emotions or capture something about life. Listen to these selections of piano music. (You can find links on my website, elizabethrusch.com.) How do they make you feel? What do they remind you of? What do they capture about life?

## Classical Music

**Ludwig van Beethoven**
Symphony No. 9, Fourth Movement, known as "Ode to Joy" (solo piano version played by David Wong)
Piano Sonata No. 14 in C-sharp minor, Op. 27, No. 2, known as the "Moonlight Sonata"

**Johannes Brahms**
"Wiegenlied" Op. 49, No. 4, known as "Brahms' Lullaby"

**Frédéric Chopin**
Prelude in A major, Op. 28, No. 7, known as "The Polish Dance"
Prelude in D-flat major, Op. 28, No. 15, known as "Raindrop"
Polonaise in A major, Op. 40, No. 1, known as "Military"
Prelude in E minor, Op. 28, No. 4

**Claude Debussy**
Suite Bergamasque No. 3, "Clair de Lune" or "Moonlight"
Preludes, Book 1, No. 6, "Footsteps in the Snow"

**Joseph Haydn**
Piano Sonata No. 50 in D major
Piano Sonata No. 52 in E-flat major

**Wolfgang Amadeus Mozart**
Piano Sonata No. 10 in C major, K. 330
Piano Sonata No. 11 in A major, K. 331

**Clara Schumann**
Piano Sonata No. 3 in G minor

## Modern Music

**Tori Amos**
"Cornflake Girl"

**Sara Bareilles**
"Brave" (Unplugged)

**Vanessa Carlton**
"A Thousand Miles"

**Coldplay**
"Clocks"

**Duke Ellington**
Piano Improvisation No. 1
"Take the A Train"

**Five for Fighting**
"100 Years"

**George Gershwin**
"Rhapsody in Blue" (piano solo version played by Vestard Simkus)

**Bruce Hornsby & the Range**
"The Way It Is"

**Elton John**
"Crocodile Rock"

**Scott Joplin**
"The Entertainer"
"The Ragtime Dance"

**Alicia Keys**
"If I Ain't Got You" (unplugged)

**Lady Gaga**
"Bad Romance/Pokerface Piano Duet Mashup" (cover by Eliza De Castro and Darcie Rehbein)

**Nirvana**
"Smells Like Teen Spirit" (cover by Eric Lewis)

**Amanda Palmer**
"Want It Back" (unplugged)

**Fats Waller**
"Ain't Misbehavin'"

**George Winston**
"Thanksgiving"

# How the Author Reconstructed Bartolomeo Cristofori's Life from Primary and Secondary Sources

Part of the joy of writing *The Music of Life* was the hunt for primary sources (handwritten notes, diary entries, newspaper articles, letters, and business records from the time) and secondary sources (books, journal articles, and even a PhD dissertation) that would help me re-create the life of someone who lived in Italy roughly three hundred years ago. Here I describe, page by page, how these treasures helped me reconstruct Bartolomeo Cristofori's story.

## Pages 4 and 5: Padua

A baptismal record from the Church of St. Luke in Padua, Italy, tells us that Bartolomeo Cristofori was born on May 4, 1655, at six a.m. The spelling of Bartolomeo's name varies in the materials I read, from Christofani and Cristofani to Cristofali but was most often written as Bartolomeo Cristofori.

Not much is known about Cristofori's life in Padua. Because his first recorded job was as instrument maker for the Medici family, historians assume that he had received extensive training in the craft.

Based on census records, some scholars believe Cristofori may have been apprenticed to Nicolò Amati, who specialized in bowed instruments. Others dismiss this idea because no bowed instruments attributed to Cristofori are mentioned in any of the inventories of Medici instruments, and the few bowed instruments bearing Cristofori's name appear to be fakes. So the issue remains unresolved.

Much of the setting and sounds in this book were inspired by descriptions in the book *Daily Life in Renaissance Italy*. In Cristofori's time, home life and work life often shared the same space, with workshops and stores in the front of a building and more private quarters in the back. Though we don't know exactly what sounds Cristofori may have heard in his house or workshop, we know that in that region and time, sand or water clocks were common and starlings were prevalent.

## Pages 6 and 7: A Prince Visits

In his book *The Early Pianoforte*, Stewart Pollens notes that the Medici's instrument maker/tuner Antonio Bolgioni died in February 1688. In an article in the journal *Early Music*, Giuliana Montanari recounts that in March or April of 1688, when Cristofori was in his thirties, twenty-five-year-old Grand Prince Ferdinando of the great Medici family of Florence stopped in Padua on his way back from attending Carnival in Venice.

We don't know much about the encounter or what the prince and the instrument maker said to each other, but we know from books like Harold Acton's *The Last Medici* that Prince Ferdinando was an accomplished horseman who traveled with a large group. Ferdinando was also a skilled harpsichordist. The excerpt on this page, from an article from the time called "History of the Noble and Royal House of the Medici" continues: "The prince possessed musical counterpoint in such a fashion that when he was in Venice and a very difficult harpsichord sonata was put in front of him, he not only played it easily at sight, but then, without looking at it again, to the amazement of all those nobles, he repeated it wondrously." Given Ferdinando's musical prowess, it's likely that the prince played one of Cristofori's harpsichords during the visit.

### Pages 8 and 9: The Invitation

In 1709, the writer Scipione Maffei interviewed Cristofori. Maffei's handwritten notes on the interview have survived. In describing the prince's invitation to join the Medici workshops, Cristofori told Maffei: "The prince was told that I did not wish to go; he replied that he would make me want to."

Next thing we know, from records in the archives of the powerful Medici family, Cristofori is on the payroll for a monthly stipend of twelve *scudi*. For his PhD dissertation, Michael O'Brien dug through all Cristofori's pay stubs. He learned that Ferdinando also paid Cristofori's rent, so his total payment averaged twenty-four *scudi* a month—more than three times what an artisan of the time might typically earn. Invoices also show Cristofori was reimbursed for materials and for work outside his main job of tuning and maintaining instruments, so he made a good living.

The prince also completely furnished Cristofori's house in Florence (according to an order given by the prince and translated by O'Brien). The detail in this list is delightful, including items like: "four domestic table cloths; twelve similar napkins; twelve tin dinner plates; four large plates, also tin; four medium-sized plates, also tin; three ladles and three forks, brass; three knives and sheath, bone" and "two small walnut tables; a small pine desk; six walnut stools with backs; eight backless stools of pine, painted green; two brass candlesticks; one large copper basin; one copper brazier; one copper kettle; one copper jug; one copper bucket with an iron lid; one copper pot; one smaller copper pot; two iron trivets; one small shovel and a pair of andirons; one iron scraper." The prince even included: "one fine pillow with a taffeta cover."

### Pages 10 and 11: Working in the Medici Workshops

Descriptions of the Medici workshops are inspired by number of books, including *Daily Life in Renaissance Italy* and *The Last Medici*. Cristofori complained about the racket in the workshops in his interview with Maffei. According to the notes: "It was very tiring for him to be in the large room with this deafening noise."

### Pages 12 and 13: Building and Restoring Instruments from Home

After 1690, invoices to the treasury of the Medici came from Cristofori's home address, suggesting he moved his shop to his house on Via agli Alberti, now known as Via de' Neri, in the St. Remigio area near the Uffizi. During a research trip to Florence, I walked this cobblestone street, wondering which of the lovely old row houses with their large wooden doors might have once been Cristofori's home and workshop.

Bills that Cristofori submitted to the Medici are translated in books such as *The Harpsichord and Clavichord: an introductory study* by Raymond Russell. The invoices were fun to read, as they included odd materials such as "fish glue," "pear-tree veneer," and "vulture feathers." But they also suggest that Cristofori was incredibly productive. From 1690 to 1698, in just eight years, Cristofori restored nine harpsichords, five spinets, and two organs, and built six harpsichords, two spinets, and one organ.

I learned about the process and steps Cristofori might have used to restore and build keyboard instruments from fascinating visits to the workshop of harpsichord maker Byron Will of Portland, Oregon, and instrument makers Tony Chinnery and Kerstin Schwarz, who have workshops in the hills outside Florence, Italy. Schwarz has made working replicas of Cristofori's keyboards and showed me the parts, the tools, and the process she—and likely Cristofori—used.

*Daily Life in Renaissance Italy* described the sounds of life at that time. The book emphasized that in cities such as Florence, church bells rang on and off all day and into the night. I heard these bells toll on my visit.

### Pages 14 and 15: The Limitations of Harpsichords and Clavichords

The dynamic limitations of these two popular keyboard instruments were well understood at the time and can be confirmed by playing the instruments today. (The volume of a clavichord *can* be changed by how hard one pushes the keys—but the volume only ranges from extremely soft to very soft.)

### Pages 16 and 17: Transporting Instruments around Florence

There are no records of what inspired Cristofori to invent the piano. But Cristofori admits to Maffei in the interview that "he learned a lot by coming here." This sent me on a journey to find out where Cristofori went and what might have inspired him. From bills submitted to the Medici, we know that Cristofori transported instruments to at least three of the prince's residences, where he was exposed to groundbreaking Renaissance and Baroque sculptures, paintings, and operas.

I visited the Pitti Palace, where stunning stone sculptures abound, especially in the Boboli Gardens. Research revealed that the prince's favorite villa outside Florence, Poggio a Caiano, displayed a remarkable collection of small paintings by great masters. The Uffizi Gallery in Florence ran an exhibition on Prince Ferdinando, which included sketches of how the prince displayed this art on his walls.

### Pages 18 and 19: Inspired by Opera

Medici invoices show that Cristofori regularly transported instruments to the Villa di Pratolino, where Prince Ferdinando put on operas every September from 1679 to 1710. Pratolino was demolished in 1820 but accounts of the lavish operas that took place are recounted in books such as *Opera Observed* by William Holmes.

### Pages 20 to 25: Inventing the Piano

As there is no record of the process Cristofori went through to invent the pianoforte, the best evidence is the instrument itself. Instrument makers such as Byron Will of Portland, Oregon, and Kerstin Schwarz and Tony Chinnery of Vicchio, Italy, know from building harpsichords and pianofortes what questions and challenges Cristofori faced. Schwarz showed me original Cristofori instruments. She took apart pieces of a replica Cristofori pianoforte she made. She even let me try out some building methods in her workshop.

Invoices submitted to the prince suggest what materials Cristofori might have tried: a variety of woods and strings, paper, felt, leather. The surviving instruments tell us what materials Cristofori ultimately chose: brass strings, cypress, paper, cloth. Finally, a diagram of the clever hammer action was published by Scipione Maffei in 1711 (and republished in 1719 and 1725) for us to study today.

### Pages 26 to 29: The Pianoforte!

While the pianoforte Cristofori built in 1700 did not survive, an incredibly detailed description of it is included in the Medici's 1700 inventory of instruments. It reads: "An *Arpicimbalo* of Bartolomeo Cristofori, of new invention, that makes the *piano* and the *forte*, with two principal stops at the unison, with cypress bottom without rose, with similar sides and half-round moldings with ebony border, with some jacks with red cloth that touch the strings and some hammers that produce the *piano* and the *forte*, and all the mechanism is closed and covered by a cypress lid bordered with ebony, with boxwood and ebony keys without split-sharps . . . with its cypress music stand, and its white spruce outer case, and its red leather cover lined with green taffeta and hemmed with golden ribbon."

While we don't know exactly how Cristofori revealed his invention, it is likely he showed it to his patron, who likely played it. We know the pianoforte was played at court because Federico Meccoli, a harpsichordist in the service of Ferdinando's father, wrote the following note about Cristofori's invention in the margins of some of his reading material: "It is possible to play both *piano* and *forte*." Prince Ferdinando's high esteem for Cristofori and his work can be found in the official list of people in his service. There he records Cristofori as a "Virtuoso of the Chamber," a high honor usually reserved for the most talented performers and composers at court.

### ❧ Pages 30 and 31: Criticism and Refinement

Two pieces of evidence prove Cristofori was not satisfied with his first pianoforte. For one, the three surviving pianofortes display changes and refinements. A primary source also suggests Cristofori's passion for perfecting his invention. The diary of Medici court musician Francesco Mannucci tells this story: "Before I left I saw Signor Cristofori rush into the Royal Chambers to speak with the prince bringing with him a key with a hammer device smaller than usual, and he told me that it was much better for striking chords with compared to the ones he himself used for the new harpsichord with *piano* and *forte*."

Cristofori never changed the basic innovation, though, that the keyboard could be played both softly and loudly. According to Maffei's article, the difficulty in playing such a sensitive instrument was the main obstacle to it catching on.

### ❧ Pages 32 and 33: Death and New Life

Cristofori's passing is noted in a number of diaries and tributes from the time, including this diary entry by Medici court musician Niccolò Susier: "1731, 27th January Bartolomeo Crisofani, called Bartolo Padovano, died, famous instrument maker to the Most Serene Grand Prince Ferdinando of fond memory, and he was a skillful maker of keyboard instruments, and also the inventor of the pianoforte, that is known through all Europe, and who served His Majesty the King of Portugal, who paid two hundred gold *louis d'or* for the said instruments." (His year of death is actually 1732 by our modern calendar.)

But Cristofori's invention lived on, in part because in 1725 the article Maffei published in Italian was translated into German and published in the journal *Critica Musica*. Experts surmise that either the article or an instrument made by Cristofori or one of his apprentices found its way to German instrument maker Gottfried Silbermann, who began making pianofortes.

### ❧ Pages 34 and 35: The Pianoforte Inspires

The accounts of the first musicians mastering the pianoforte are inspiring. Joseph Haydn remarked to his biographer: "I sat down, began to improvise, according to my mood, sad or happy, serious or playful. Once I had seized upon an idea, my entire effort went toward putting it into effect and sustaining it according to the rules of art. . . . If it's an *allegro* that persecutes me then my pulse beats harder and harder, I can't sleep. If it's an *adagio* then I notice that my pulse beats slowly. My imagination plays on me as if I were a keyboard. . . . I am really just a living keyboard."

As the pianoforte became more popular, musicians began to play the instrument in public, and audiences were thrilled. The excerpt of the article from the Augsburg newspaper on these pages captured beautifully people's reaction to one of Wolfgang Mozart's first concerts with the instrument.

After the 1780s, most keyboard composers embraced the pianoforte. From that time on, dynamic markings such as *piano* and *forte* became so commonplace on written keyboard music that it is hard to imagine playing a piece without varying the volume.

# Bibliography

Acton, Harold. *The Last Medici*. New York: Thames and Hudson, 1980.

Chinnery, Tony. Italian harpsichord builder, Vicchio, Italy. Author visit to workshop. Summer 2012.

Cohen, Elizabeth S. and Thomas V. *Daily Life in Renaissance Italy*. Westport, CT: Greenwood Press, 2001.

Deutsch, Otto Erich. *Mozart: A Documentary Biography*. Stanford: Stanford University Press, 1965.

Halton, Rosalind. Associate Professor of Music at the University of Newcastle, Australia. E-mails with author 2014.

Holmes, William C. *Opera Observed: Views of a Florentine Impresario in the Early Eighteenth Century*. Chicago: University of Chicago Press, 1993.

Kraaz, Sarah. Professor of Music, Ripon College, Ripon, Wisconsin. E-mails with the author 2014.

O'Brien, Michael Kent. *Bartolomeo Cristofori at Court in Late Medici Florence*. Washington, D.C.: Catholic University of America, 1994.

Montanari, Giuliana. "Bartolomeo Cristofori: A list and historical survey of his instruments," *Early Music*, Vol. 19, No. 3 (Aug. 1991) pp. 383–396.

Pagano, Roberto. *Alessandro and Domenico Scarlatti: Two Lives in One*. Translated by Frederick Hammond. Hillsdale, NY: Pendragon Press, 2006.

Pollens, Stewart. *The Early Pianoforte*. Cambridge: Cambridge University Press, 1995.

Russell, Raymond. *The Harpsichord and Clavichord: An Introductory Study*. New York: October House, 1965.

Schwarz, Kerstin. Builder of replica Cristofori pianofortes, Vicchio, Italy. Guided visit to the Museum of Musical Instruments in the Accademia Gallery in Florence and to her workshop in Vicchio, Italy, and e-mail discussions. Summer 2012–2014.

Sisman, Elaine. "Haydn's Solo Keyboard Music," in *Eighteenth-Century Keyboard Music*, edited by Robert L. Marshall. New York: Schirmer Books, 1994.

Spinelli, Riccardo. *The Grand Prince Ferdinando de' Medici and Anton Domenico Gabbiani*. Florence: Noedizione, 2003.

Surace, Ron. "Cristofori, Bartolomeo (1655-1732)." in *Piano: An Encyclopedia Second Edition*, edited by Robert Palmieri, associate editor Margaret W. Palmieri. New York: Routledge, 2003.

Will, Byron. Harpsichord maker, Portland, Oregon. Author visit to workshop and e-mail and phone discussions. June 2012.

Wraight, Denzil. Builder and restorer of Italian keyboard instruments, including Cristofori instruments, Naumburg, Germany. E-mail correspondences, 2014.

Wraight, Denzil. "Recent Approaches in Understanding Cristofori's Fortepiano." *Early Music* (Oxford University Press) 34, no. 4 (August 2006): 635–644.

# Sources for Quotations

**4:** *Bartolomeo, son of Francesco . . .* O'Brien, p. 2.

**7:** *[Prince Ferdinando] played various . . .* Pagano, quoting the anonymous *History of the Noble and Royal House of the Medici*, p. 50.

**8:** *The prince was told . . .* O'Brien, p. 69 and Montanari, p. 384.

**9:** *To Bartolomeo . . .* O'Brien, pp. 184–185.

**11:** *It was very tiring . . .* Pollens, p. 234.

**12:** *I, Bartolomeo . . .* Russell, p. 127.

**16:** *Owed to me . . .* Russell, p. 126.

**19:** *The opera was rehearsed . . .* Holmes, p. 27.

**26:** *[A] new invention, that makes the piano . . .* Montanari, p. 391.

**29:** *It is possible to play . . .* Montanari, p. 385.

**29:** *Virtuoso . . .* Montanari, p. 386.

**31:** *But truly, the major . . .* Pollens, p. 58.

**33:** *Constructing [a keyboard] so that it . . .* Pollens, p. 57.

**34:** *My imagination plays . . .* Sisman, p. 270.

**35:** *The rendering on the . . .* Deutsch, p. 168.

**43:** *The prince possessed musical . . .* Pagano, p. 50.

**44:** *The Prince was told . . .* Montanari, p. 384.

**44:** *four domestic table cloths . . . with a taffeta cover*, O'Brien, pp. 184–186.

**44:** *It was very tiring . . .* Pollens, p. 234.

**44:** *fish glue . . . vulture feathers . . .* Russell, pp. 126–127.

**45:** *he learned a lot . . .* Montanari, p. 384.

**45:** *An Arpicimbalo of Bartolomeo . . .* Montanari, p. 391.

**46:** *It is possible . . .* Montanari, p. 385.

**46:** *Virtuoso . . .* O'Brien, p. 55

**46:** *Before I left . . .* Montanari, p. 386.

**46:** *1731, 27th January . . .* Pollens, p. 55.

**46:** *I sat down . . .* Sisman, p. 270.